F*CK

Swear Words
Coloring Book for Adult

By

S.B. Nozaz

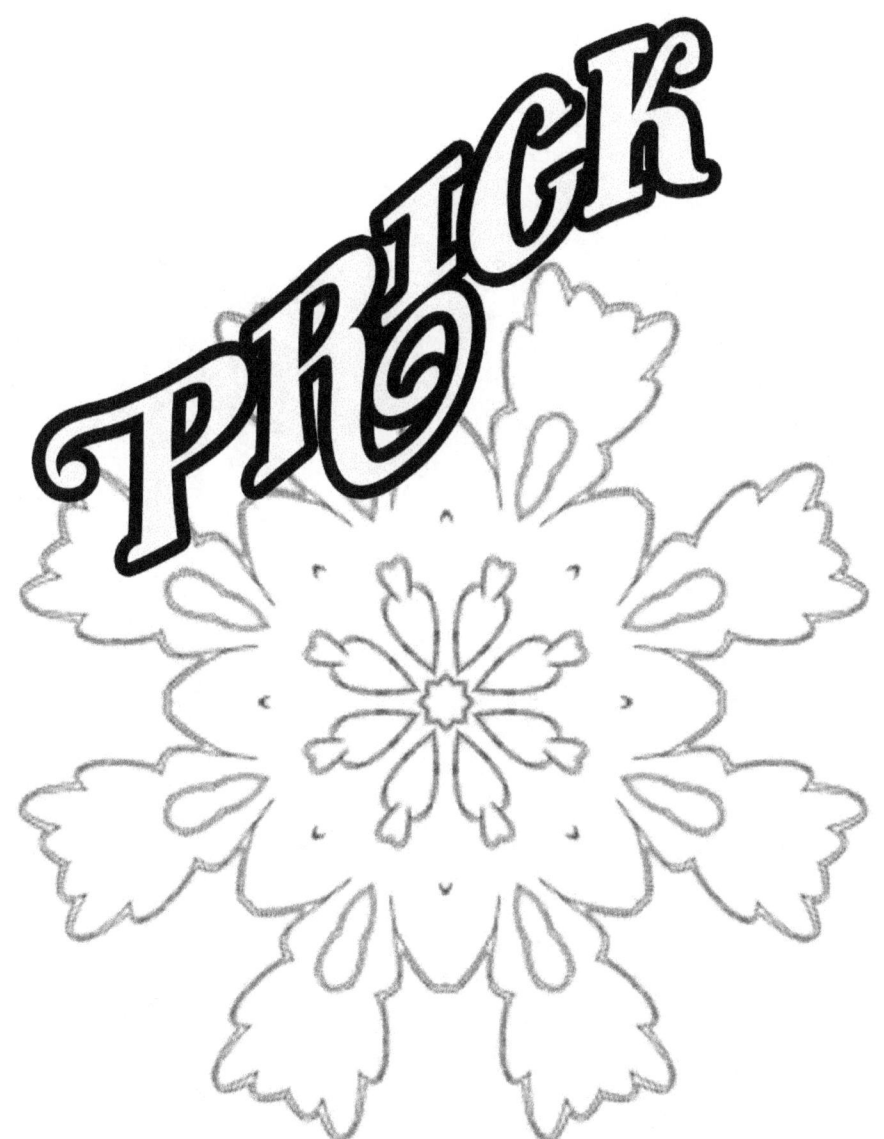

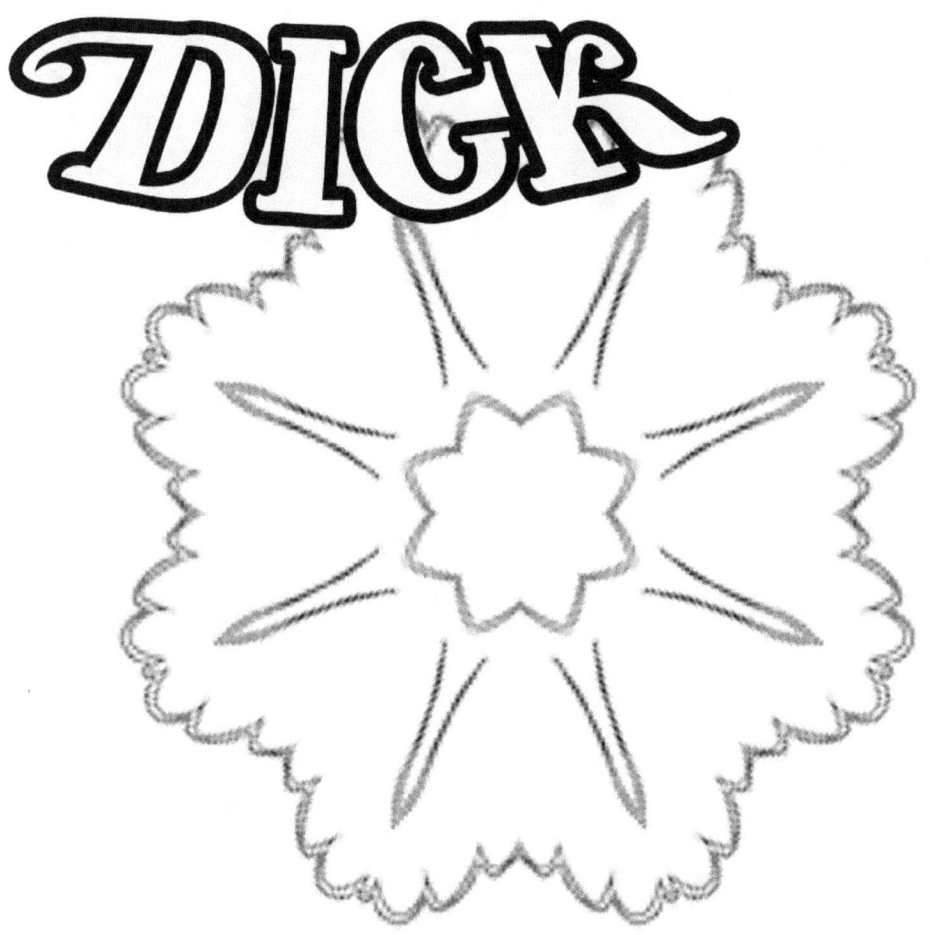

ASSHOLE

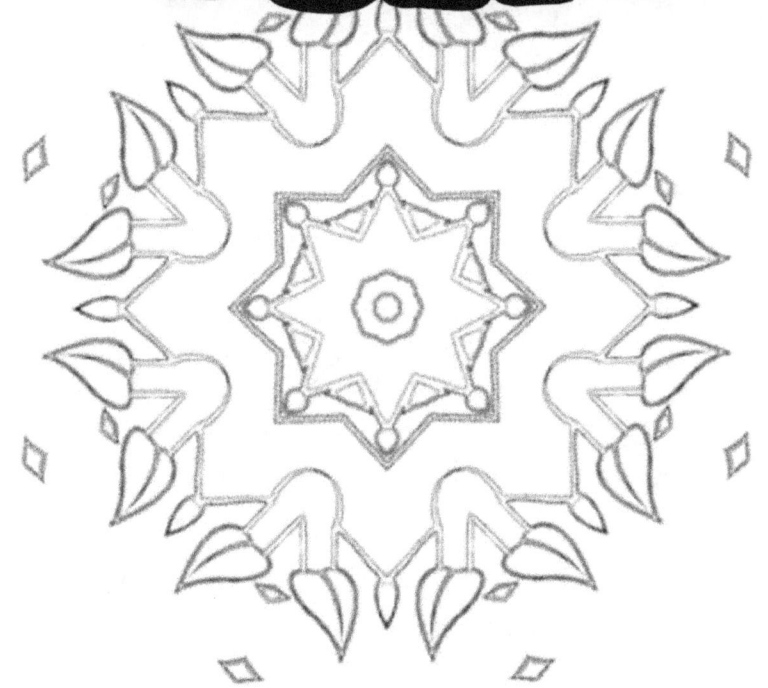

ASS

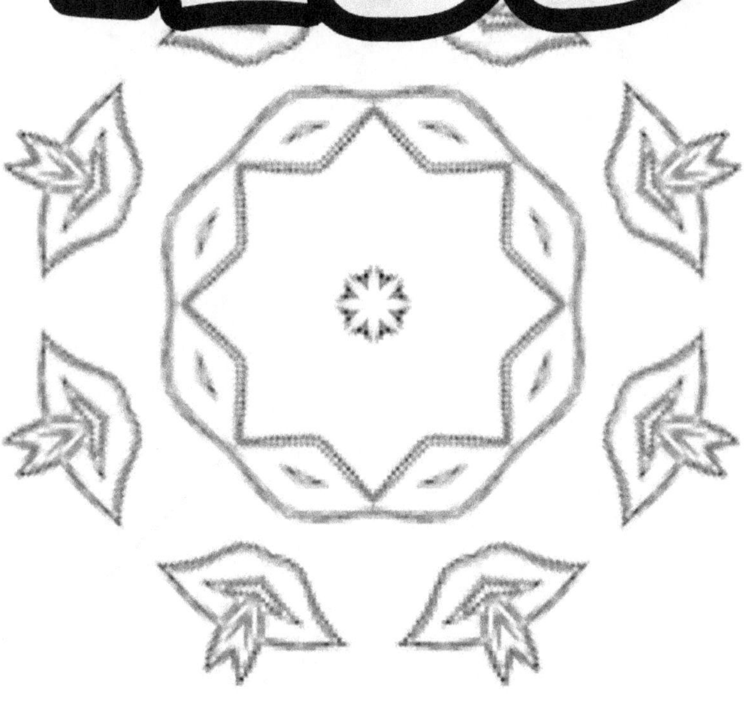

DOUCHEBAG

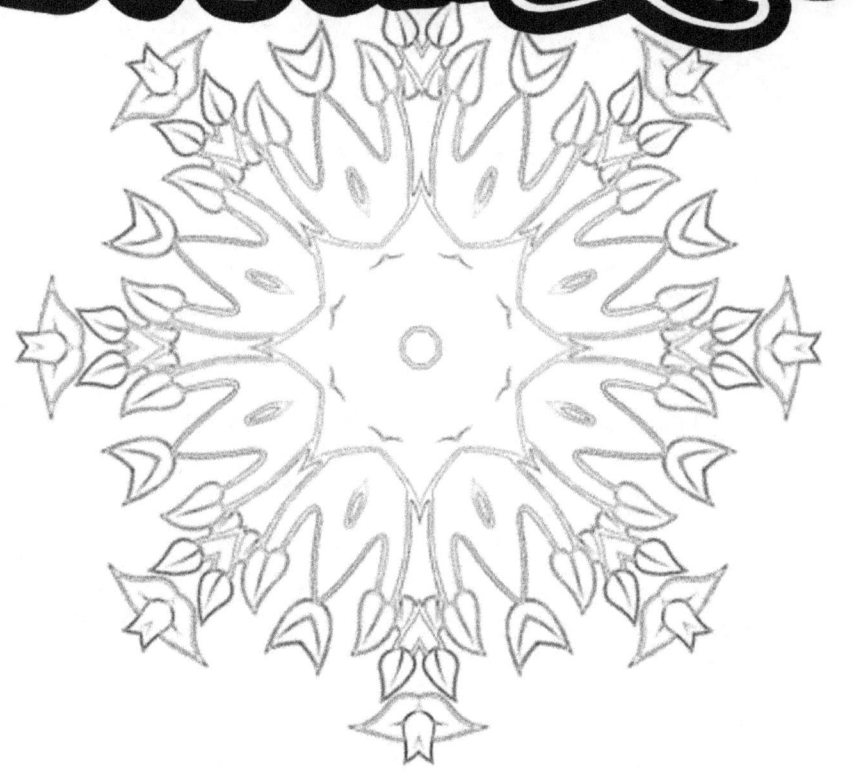

FUCK UP

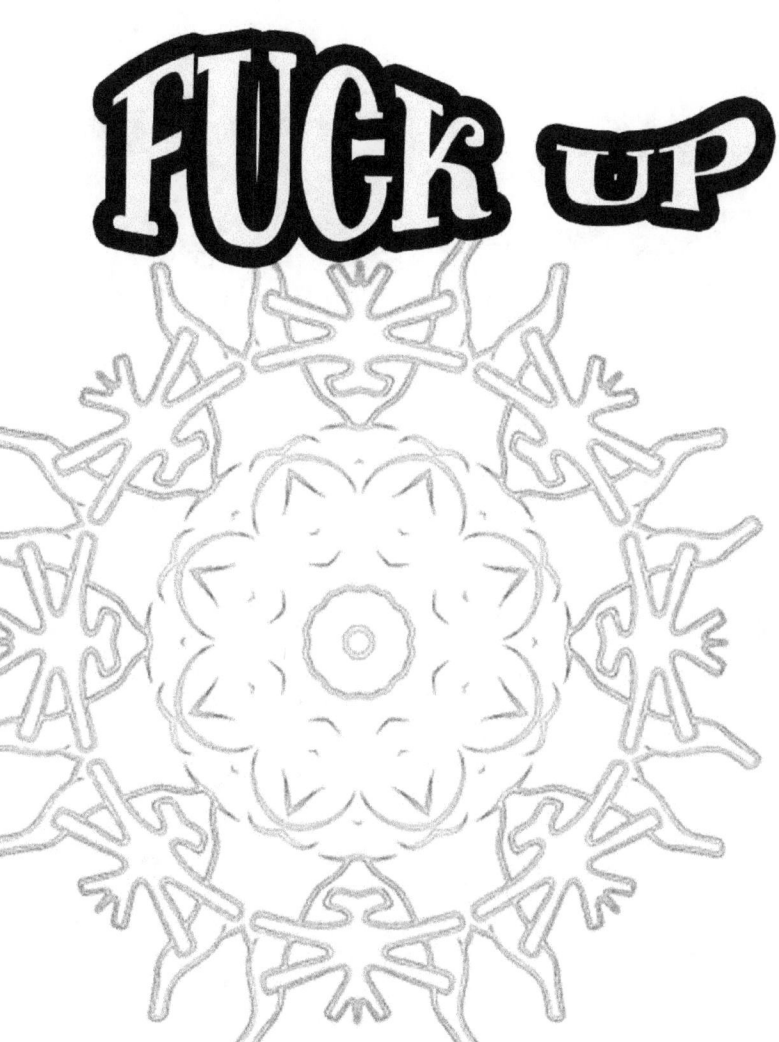

MOTHER FUCKER

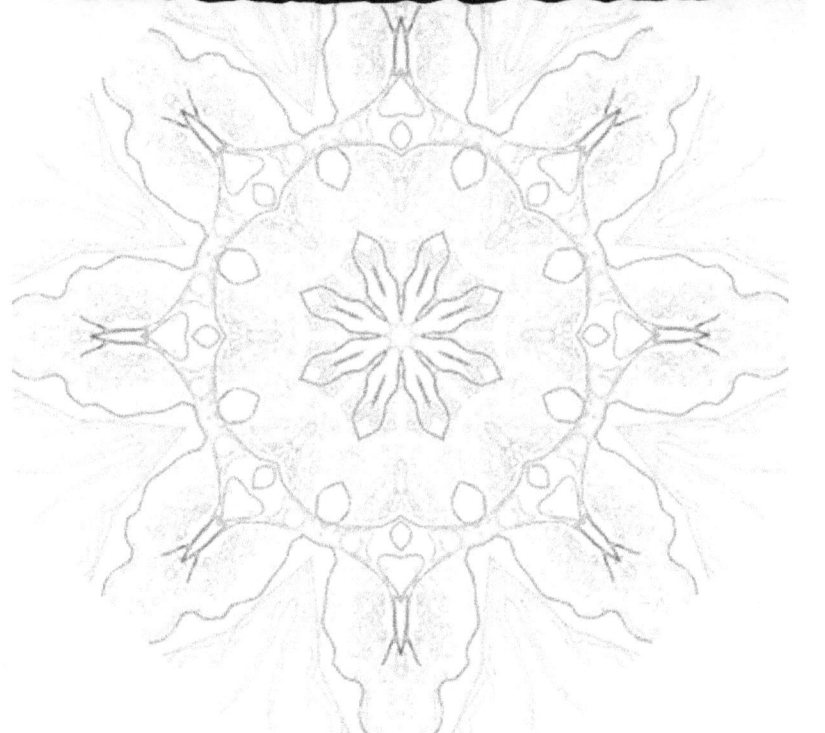

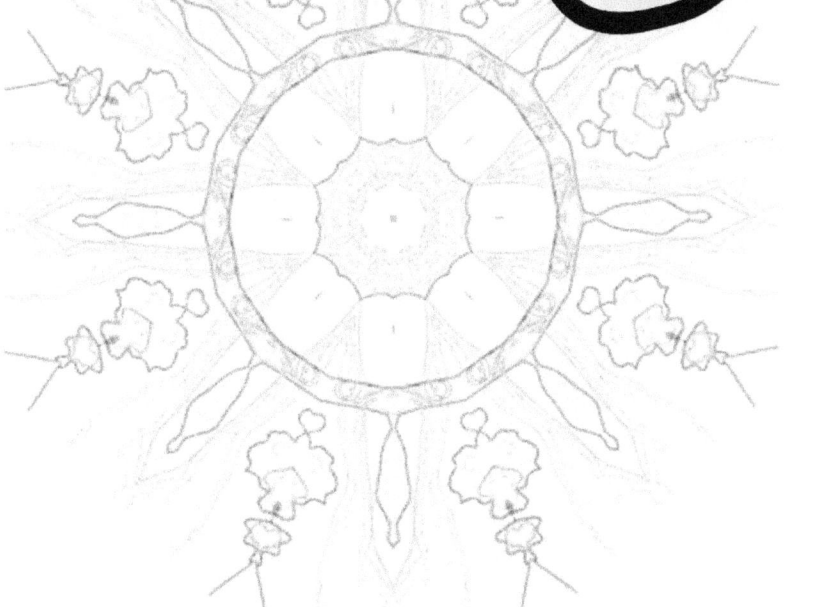

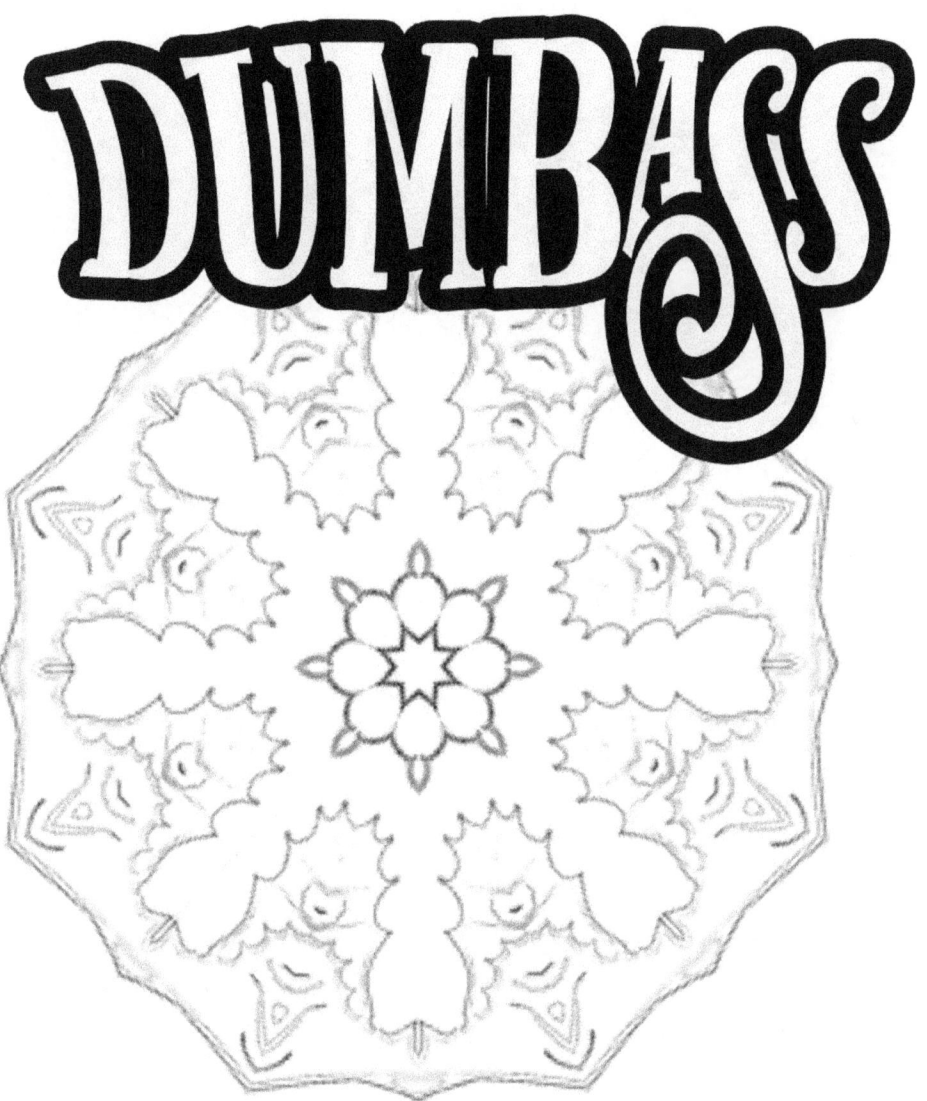

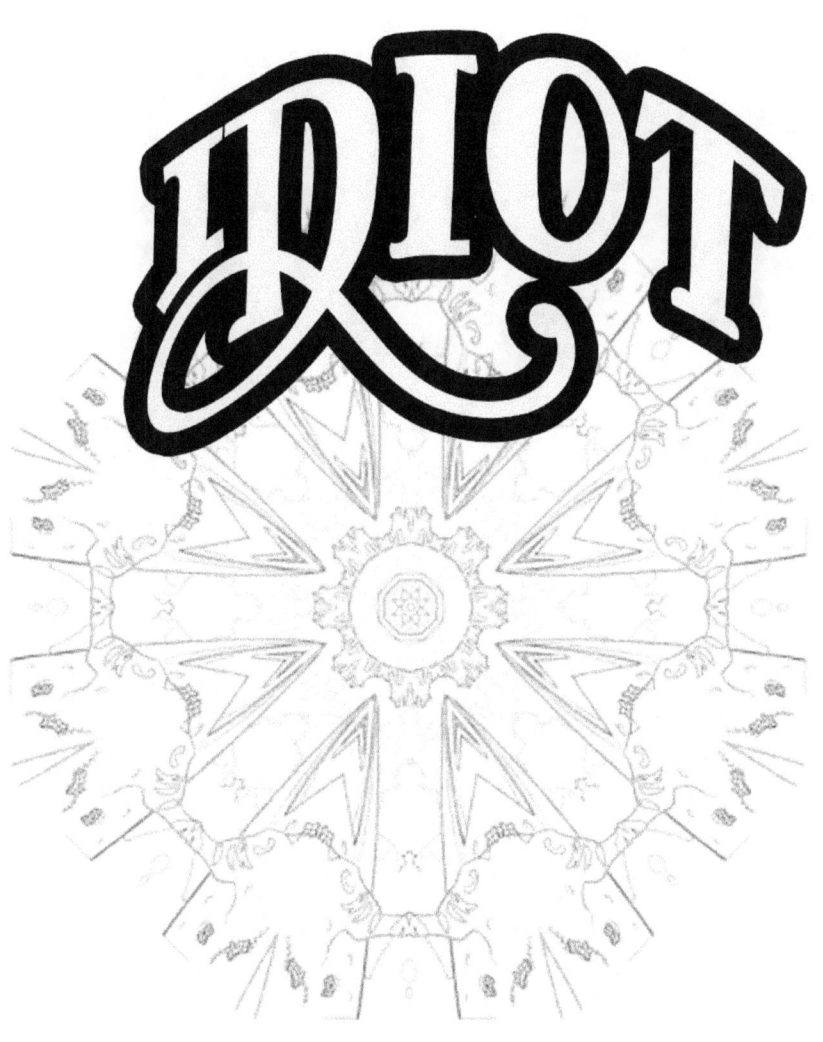

PIECE

OF

SHIT

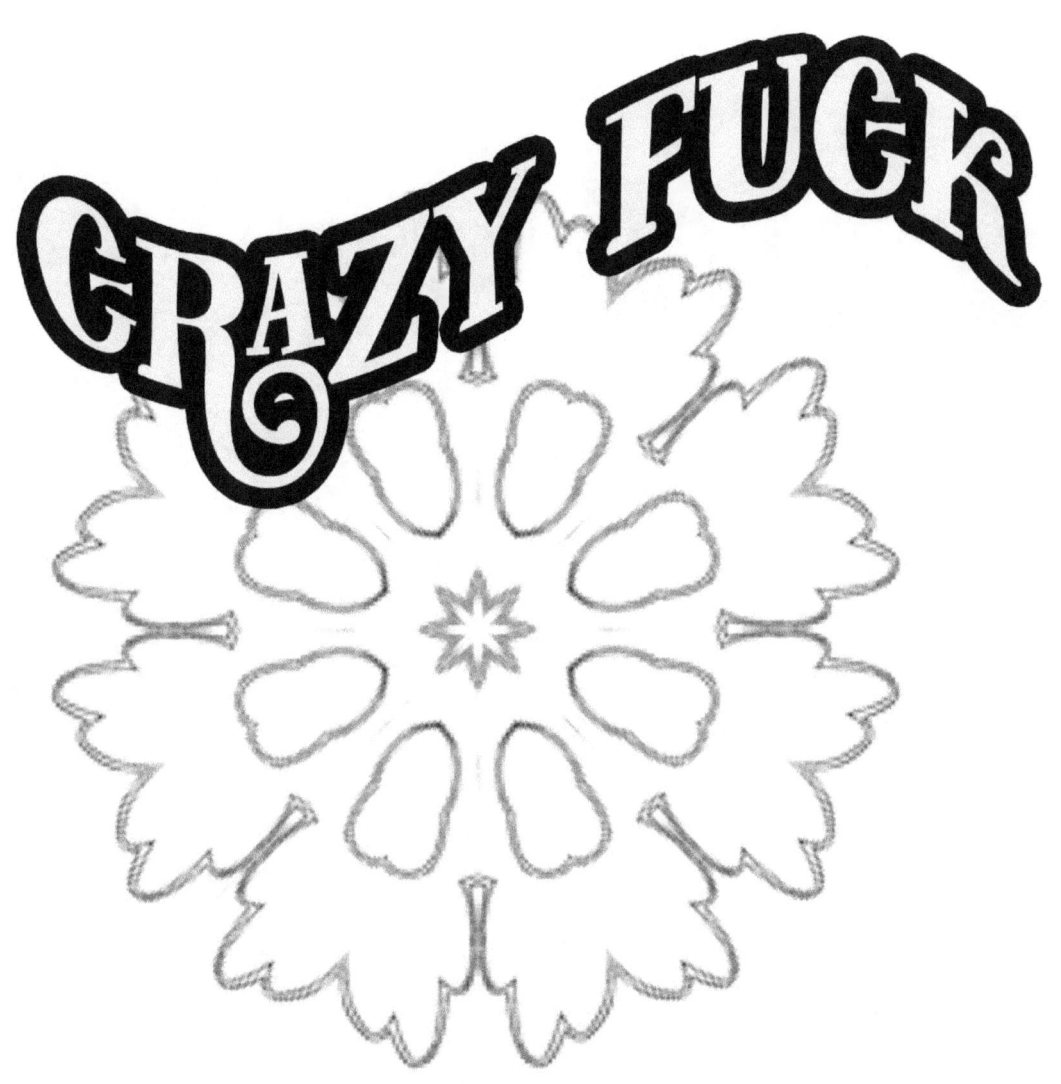

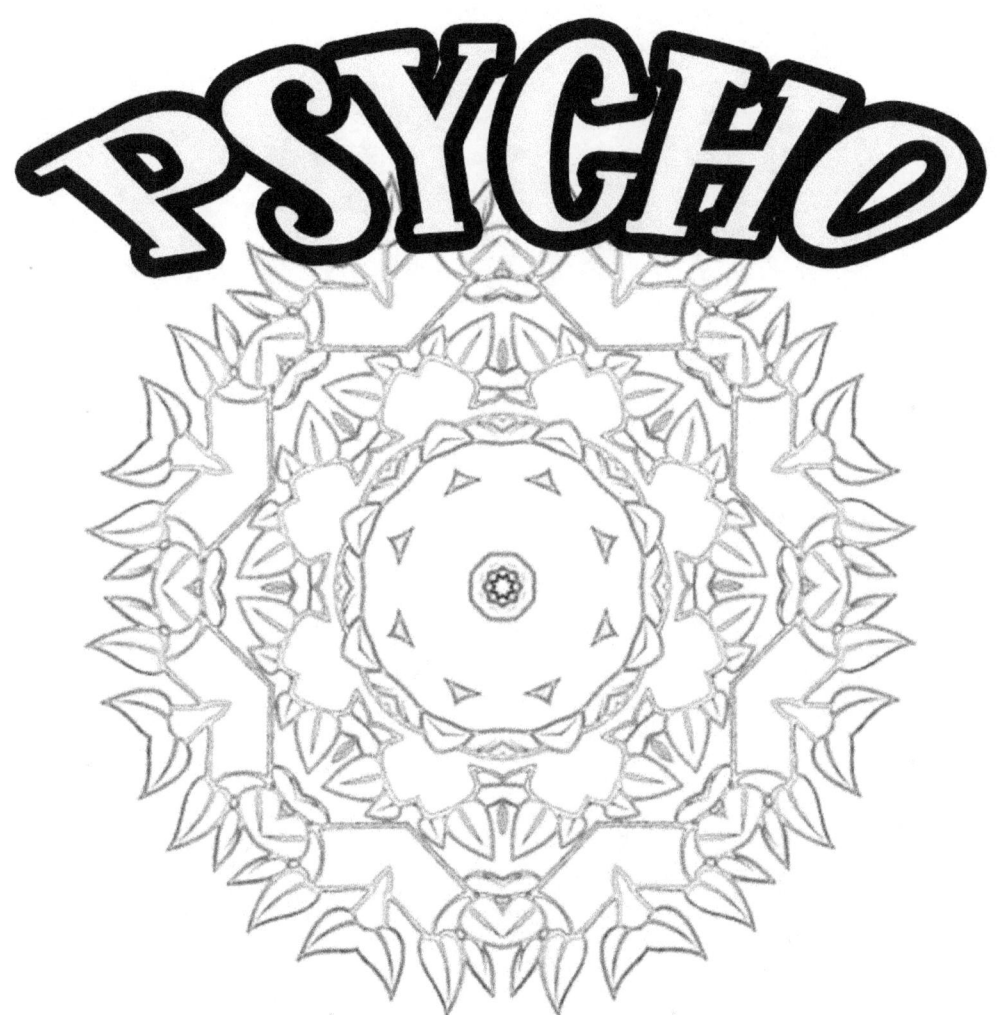

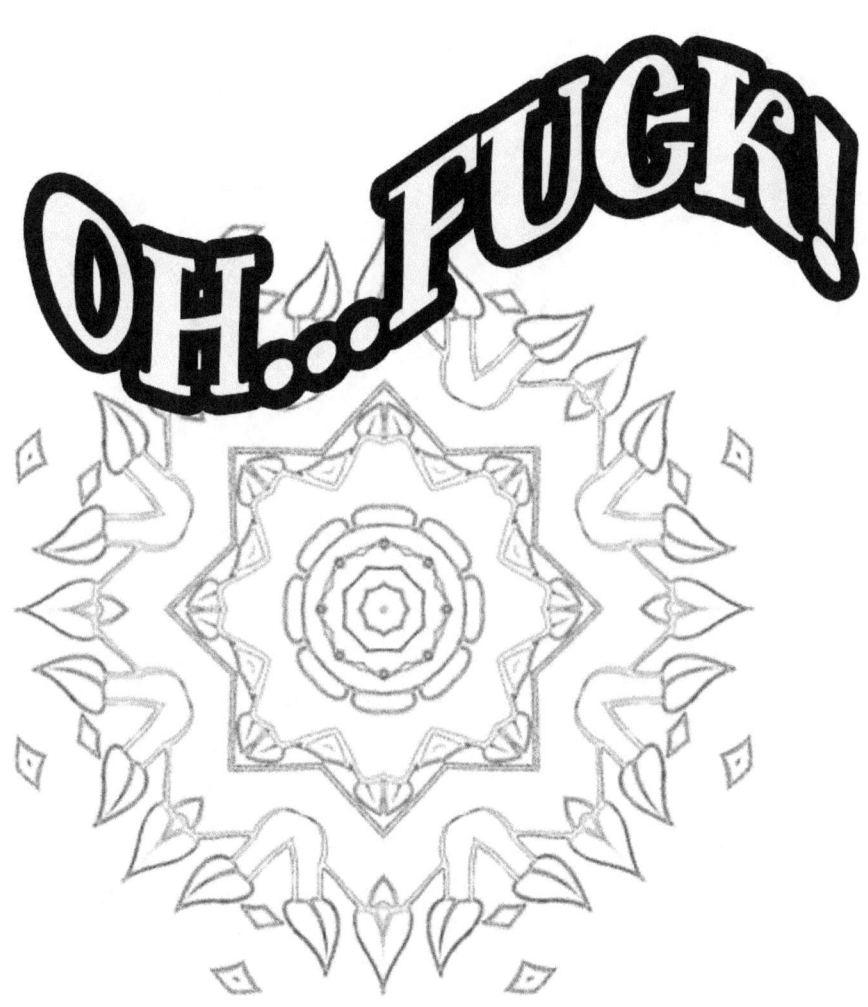

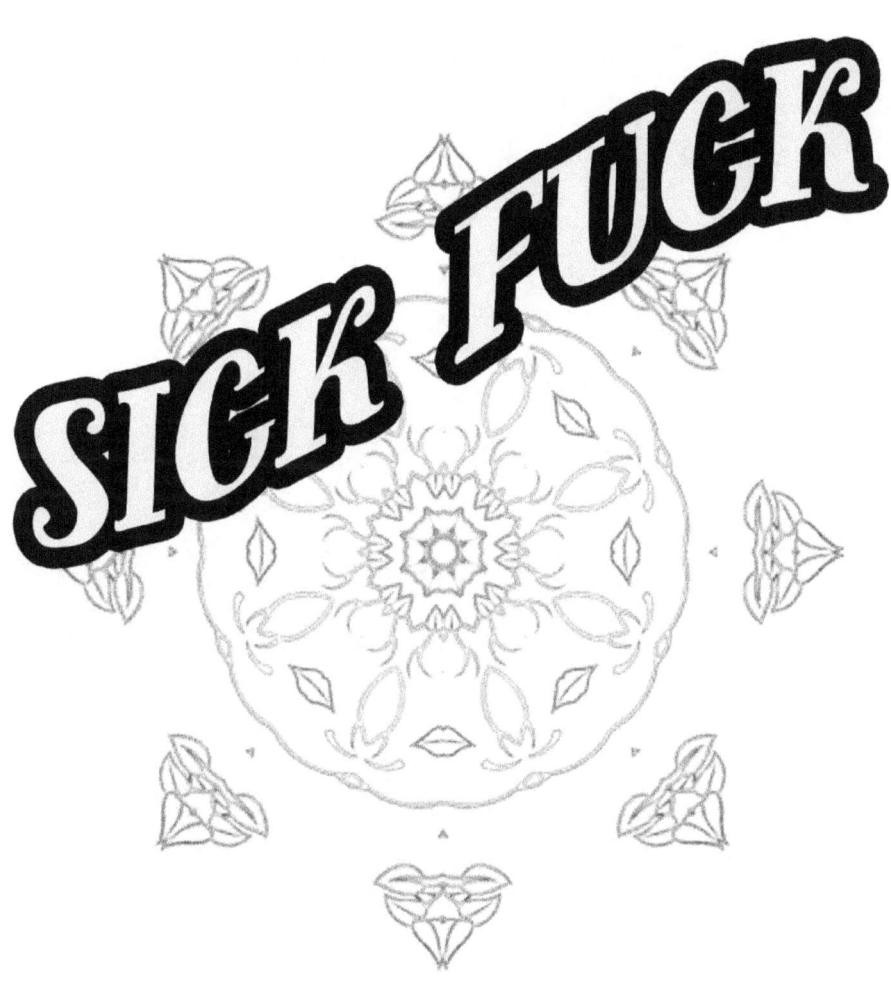

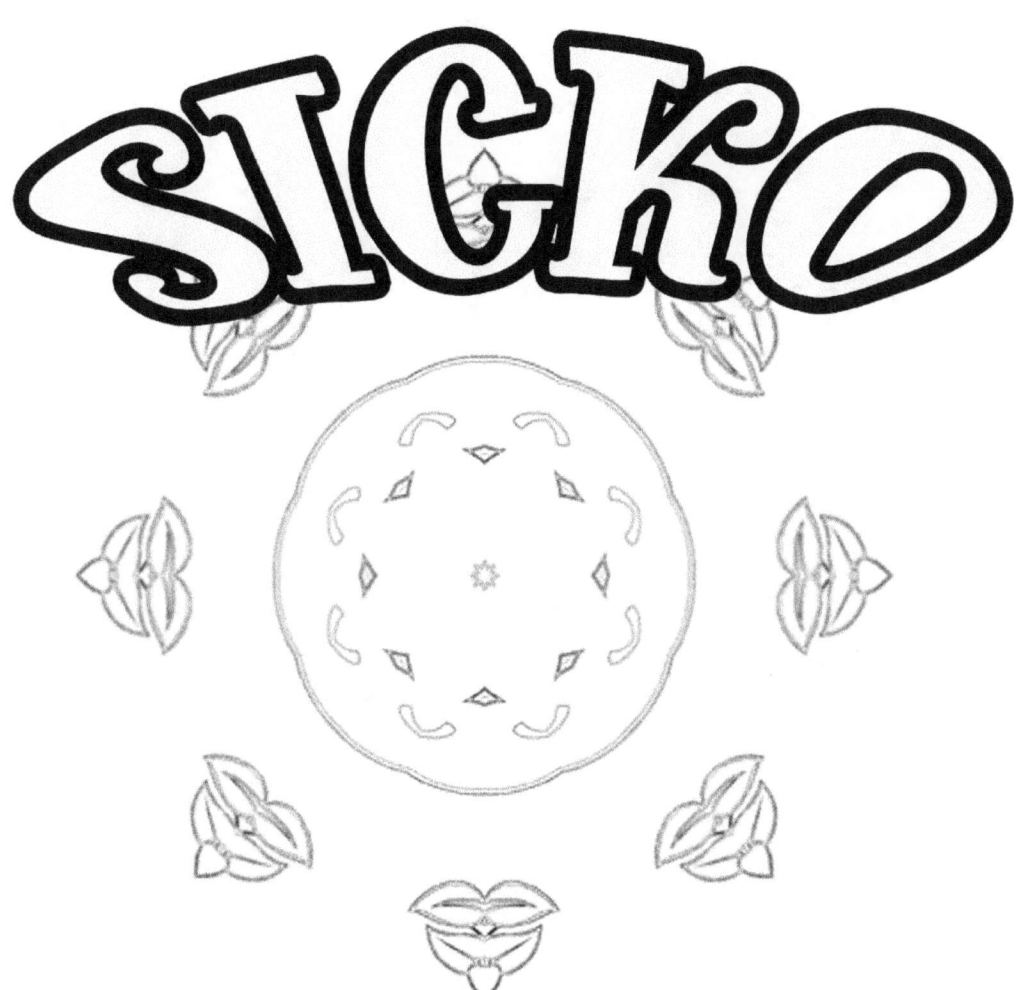

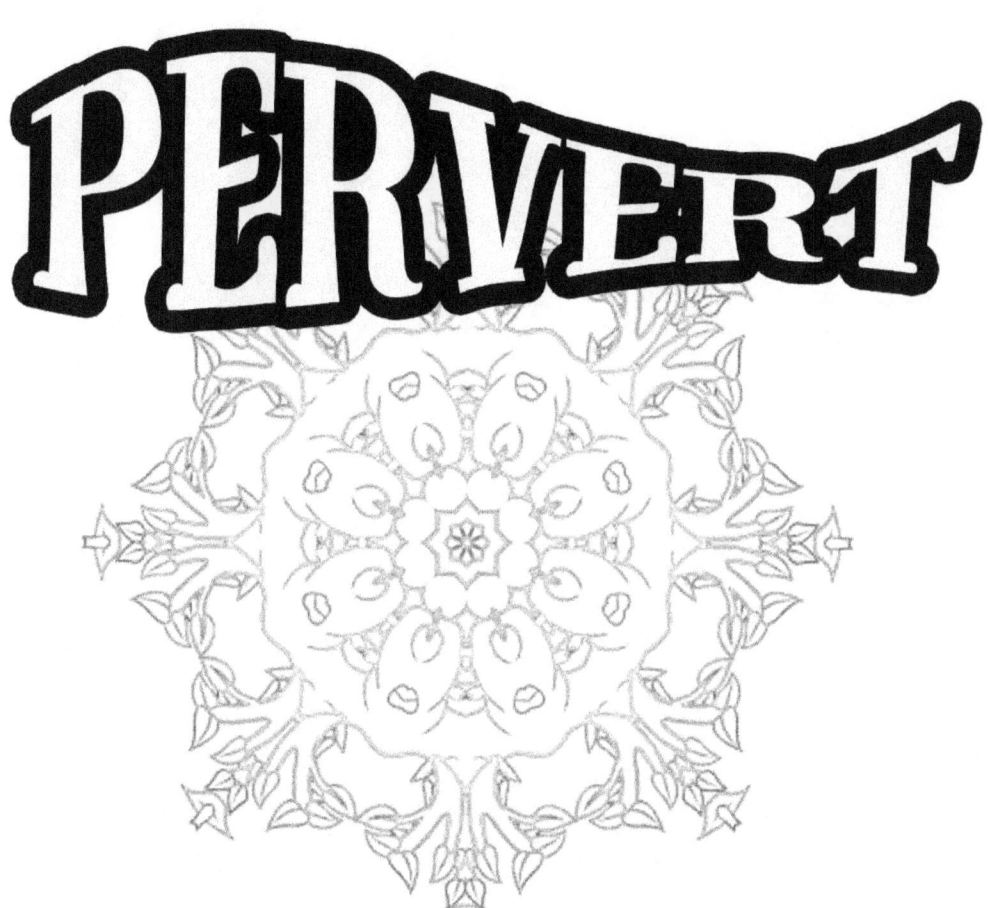

PERVERT

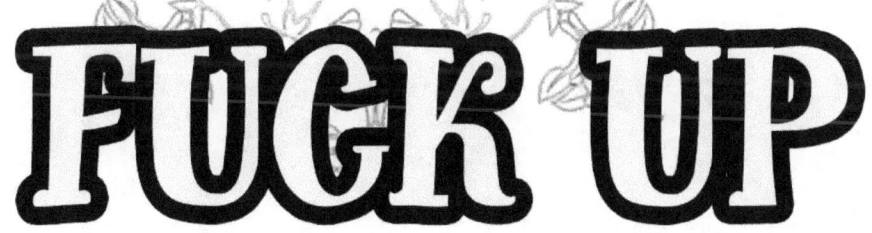

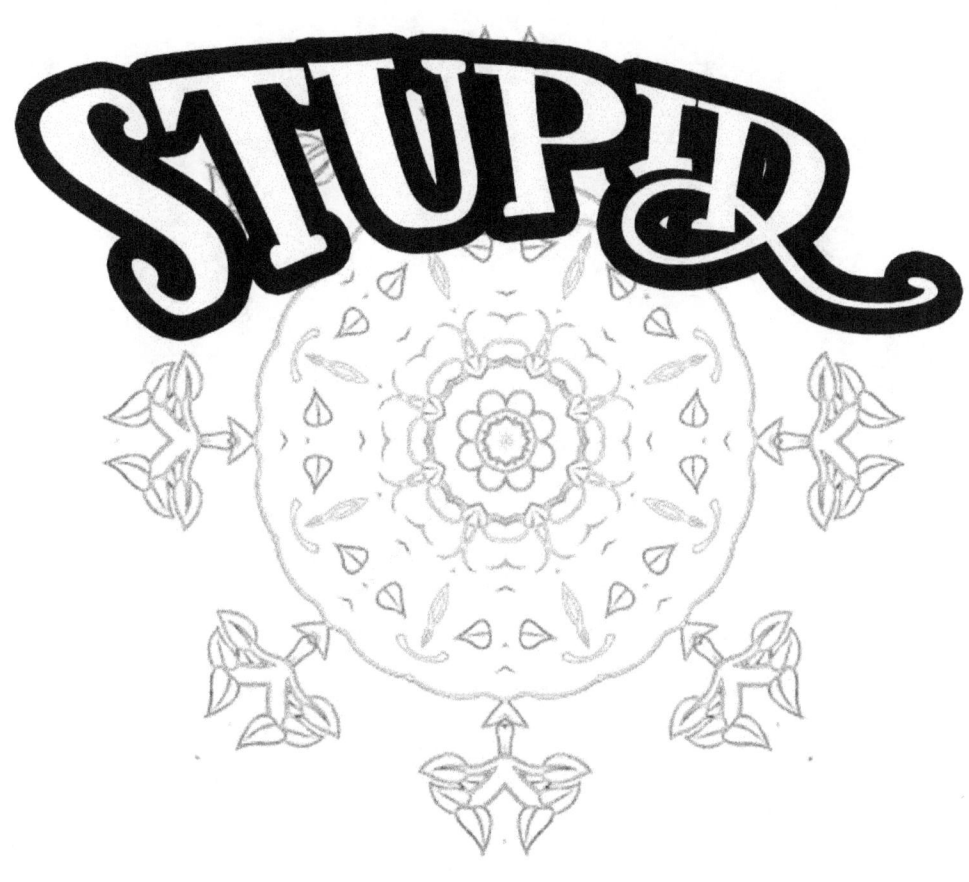

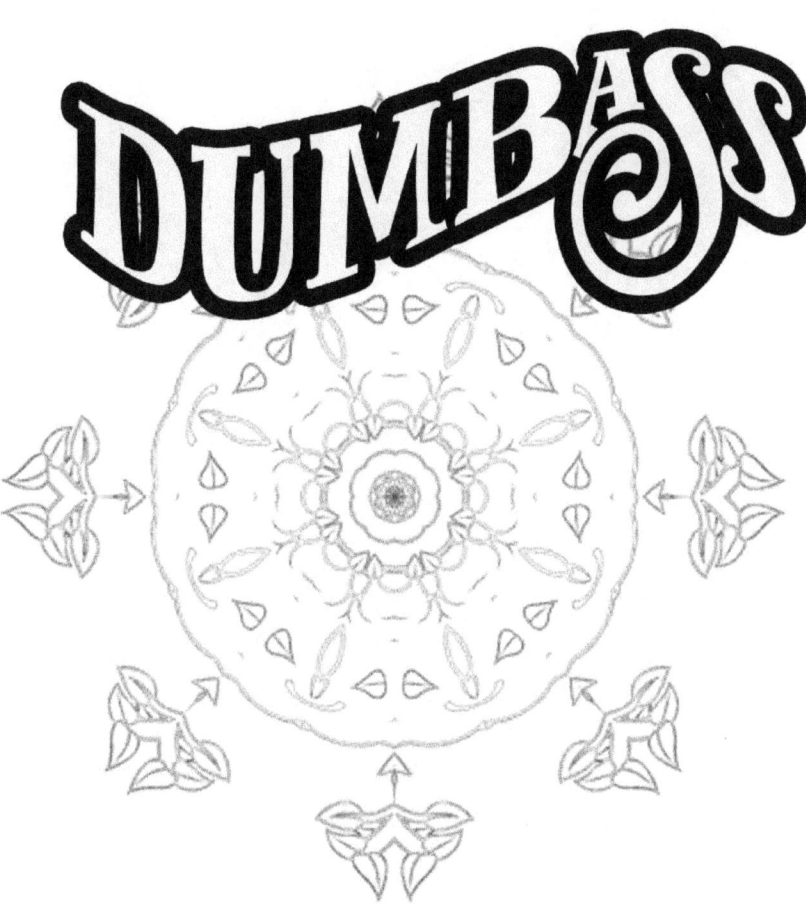

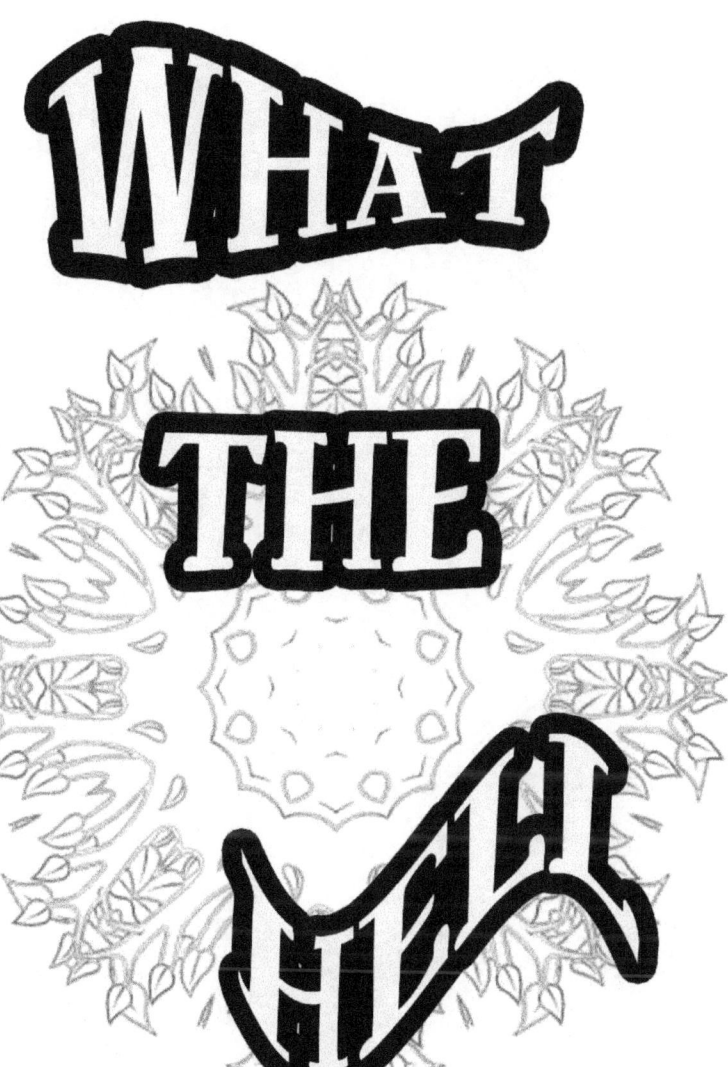

WHAT THE HECK

GO TO
FUCK
YOURSELF

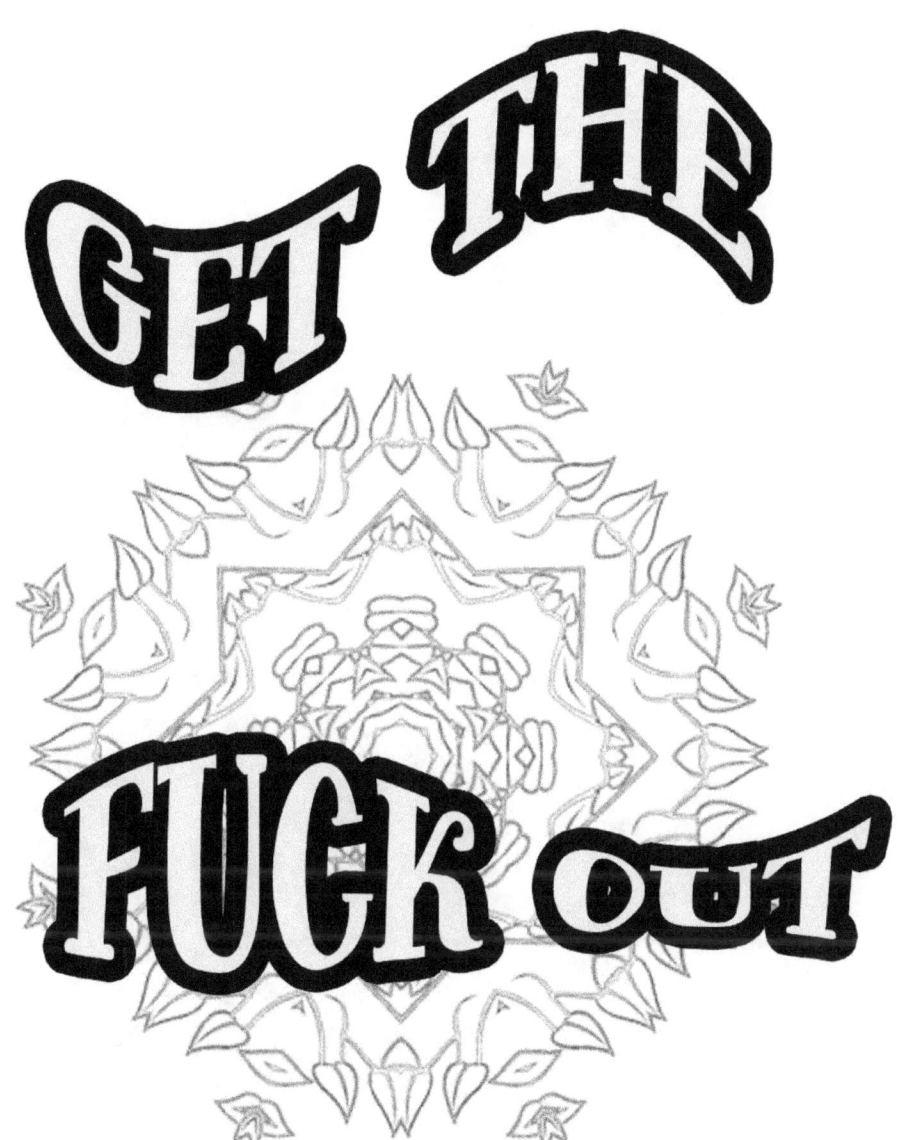

www.ingramcontent.com/pod-product-compliance
Lightning Source LLC
Chambersburg PA
CBHW080641190526

45169CB00009B/3460